"It's hard to connect with your child without first understanding where they are. As counselors and speakers at parenting events across the country, we spend a great deal of time teaching parents about development. To know *where* your child is—not just physically, but emotionally, socially, and spiritually, helps you to truly know and understand *who* your child is. And that understanding is the key to connecting. The Phase Guides give you the tools to do just that. Our wise friends Reggie and Kristen have put together an insightful, hopeful, practical, and literal year-by-year guide that will help you to understand and connect with your child at every age."

### SISSY GOFF
*M.ED., LPC-MHSP, DIRECTOR OF CHILD & ADOLESCENT COUNSELING AT DAYSTAR COUNSELING MINISTRIES IN NASHVILLE, TENNESSEE, SPEAKER AND AUTHOR OF ARE MY KIDS ON TRACK?*

"These resources for parents are fantastically empowering, absolute in their simplicity, and completely doable in every way. The hard work that has gone into the Phase Project will echo through the next generation of children in powerful ways."

### JENNIFER WALKER
*RN BSN, AUTHOR AND FOUNDER OF MOMS ON CALL*

"We all know where we want to end up in our parenting, but how to get there can seem like an unsolved mystery. Through the Phase Project series, Reggie Joiner and Kristen Ivy team up to help us out. The result is a resource that guides us through the different seasons of raising children, and provides a road map to parenting in such a way that we finish up with very few regrets."

### SANDRA STANLEY
*FOSTER CARE ADVOCATE, BLOGGER, WIFE TO ANDY STANLEY, MOTHER OF THREE*

"Not only are the Phase Guides the most creative and well-thought-out guides to parenting I have ever encountered, these books are ESSENTIAL to my daily parenting. With a 13-year-old, 11-year-old, and 9-year-old at home, I am swimming in their wake of daily drama and delicacy. These books are a reminder to enjoy every second. Because it's just a phase."

### CARLOS WHITTAKER
*AUTHOR, SPEAKER, FATHER OF THREE*

"As the founder of Minnie's Food Pantry, I see thousands of people each month with children who will benefit from the advice, guidance, and nuggets of information on how to celebrate and understand the phases of their child's life. Too often we feel like we're losing our mind when sweet little Johnny starts to change his behavior into a person we do not know. I can't wait to start implementing the principles of these books with my clients to remind them . . . it's just a phase."

### CHERYL JACKSON
*FOUNDER OF MINNIE'S FOOD PANTRY, AWARD-WINNING PHILANTHROPIST, AND GRANDMOTHER*

"I began exploring this resource with my counselor hat on, thinking how valuable this will be for the many parents I spend time with in my office. I ended up taking my counselor hat off and putting on my parent hat. Then I kept thinking about friends who are teachers, coaches, youth pastors, and children's ministers, who would want this in their hands. What a valuable resource the Orange team has given us to better understand and care for the kids and adolescents we love. I look forward to sharing it broadly."

**DAVID THOMAS**
*LMSW, DIRECTOR OF FAMILY COUNSELING, DAYSTAR COUNSELING MINISTRIES, SPEAKER AND AUTHOR OF ARE MY KIDS ON TRACK? AND WILD THINGS: THE ART OF NURTURING BOYS*

"I have always wished someone would hand me a manual for parenting. Well, the Phase Guides are more than what I wished for. They guide, inspire, and challenge me as a parent—while giving me incredible insight into my children at each age and phase. Our family will be using these every year!"

**COURTNEY DEFEO**
*AUTHOR OF IN THIS HOUSE, WE WILL GIGGLE, MOTHER OF TWO*

"As I speak to high school students and their parents, I always wonder to myself: What would it have been like if they had better seen what was coming next? What if they had a guide that would tell them what to expect and how to be ready? What if they could anticipate what is predictable about the high school years before they actually hit? These Phase Guides give a parent that kind of preparation so they can have a plan when they need it most."

**JOSH SHIPP**
*AUTHOR, TEEN EXPERT, AND YOUTH SPEAKER*

"The Phase Guides are incredibly creative, well researched, and filled with inspirational actions for everyday life. Each age-specific guide is catalytic for equipping parents to lead and love their kids as they grow up. I'm blown away and deeply encouraged by the content and by its creators. I highly recommend Phase resources for all parents, teachers, and influencers of children. This is the stuff that challenges us and changes our world. Get them. Read them. And use them!"

**DANIELLE STRICKLAND**
*OFFICER WITH THE SALVATION ARMY, AUTHOR, SPEAKER, MOTHER OF TWO*

"It's true that parenting is one of life's greatest joys but it is not without its challenges. If we're honest, parenting can sometimes feel like trying to choreograph a dance to an ever-changing beat. It can be clumsy and riddled with well-meaning missteps. If parenting is a dance, this Parenting Guide is a skilled instructor refining your technique and helping you move gracefully to a steady beat. For those of us who love to plan ahead, this guide will help you anticipate what's to come so you can be poised and ready to embrace the moments you want to enjoy."

**TINA NAIDOO**
*MSSW, LCSW EXECUTIVE DIRECTOR, THE POTTER'S HOUSE OF DALLAS, INC.*

# PARENTING YOUR THREE-YEAR-OLD

## A GUIDE TO MAKING THE MOST OF THE "WHY?" PHASE

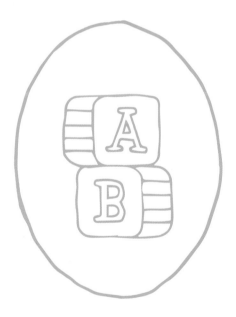

KRISTEN IVY AND REGGIE JOINER

# PARENTING YOUR THREE-YEAR-OLD
## A GUIDE TO MAKING THE MOST OF THE
## "WHY?" PHASE

Published by Orange, a division of The reThink Group, Inc.,
5870 Charlotte Lane, Suite 300,
Cumming, GA 30040 U.S.A.

©2017 Kristen Ivy and Reggie Joiner
Authors: Kristen Ivy and Reggie Joiner
Lead Editor: Karen Wilson
Editing Team: Melanie Williams, Hannah Crosby, Sherry Surratt

Art Direction: Ryan Boon and Hannah Crosby
Book Design: FiveStone and Sharon van Rossum

Printed in the United States of America
First Edition 2017
1 2 3 4 5 6 7 8 9 10

*Special thanks to:*

*Jim Burns, Ph.D for guidance and consultation on having conversations about sexual integrity*

*Jon Acuff for guidance and consultation on having conversations about technological responsibility*

*Jean Sumner, MD for guidance and consultation on having conversations about healthy habits*

*Every educator, counselor, community leader, and researcher who invested in the Phase Project*

# TABLE OF CONTENTS

# HOW TO USE THIS ~~BOOK~~ ~~JOURNAL~~ GUIDE

The guide you hold in your hand doesn't have very many words, but it does have a lot of ideas. Some of these ideas come from thousands of hours of research. Others come from parents, educators, and volunteers who spend every day with kids the same age as yours. This guide won't tell you everything about your kid, but it will tell you a few things about kids at this age.

The best way to use this guide is to take what these pages tell you about preschoolers and combine it with what you know is true about your preschooler.

Let's sum it up:

**THINGS ABOUT PRESCHOOLERS +**
**THOUGHTS ABOUT YOUR PRESCHOOLER =**
**YOUR GUIDE TO THE NEXT 52 WEEKS OF PARENTING**

After each idea in this guide, there are pages with a few questions designed to prompt you to think about your kid, your family, and yourself as a parent. The only guarantee we give to parents who use this guide is this: You will mess up some things as a parent this year. Actually, that's a guarantee to every parent, regardless. But you, you picked up this book! You want to be a better parent. And that's what we hope this guide will do: help you parent your preschooler just a little better, simply because you paused to consider a few ideas that can help you make the most of this phase.

# THE THREE-YEAR-OLD PHASE

If you ask me, any phase that involves sleeping through the night is far superior to any that don't. Add uninterrupted REM to the fact that most three-year-olds are beginning to learn how to dress themselves, go to the bathroom in an actual toilet, and tell you what they want for dinner (granted, it's usually chicken nuggets). A parent may get to this phase and think: *Whew. Those first three years were nuts. Now maybe I can relax a little.* Right?

No, parents. Not right. Because just about the time you sit down on your sofa for the first time in three years, your child's brain starts to rev its engine. And the questions begin.

How does a computer work?
Why does your hair look so fuzzy?
Why do you have to go to work again today?
Why do jaguars live in the Amazon rainforest and not in the woods behind our house? (Thanks, Dora the Explorer.)

And, one of my personal favorites asked by my own daughter:

If you're not pregnant, why does it look like you have a baby in your belly?

This is the age of wonder. This is the age of curiosity. This is the age when anything and everything is possible. And it's the best age of them all, because through your child's inquisitions, you experience the world in a new way. You see the sky differently. You see technology differently. You see yourself differently.

I remember a conversation I had with my daughter when she was three years old. She was asking me questions about God. "Mom, where does God live? Mom, does God have a bedtime? Mom, does God cheer for the University of Tennessee?" I was driving in my car—my thoughts scattered in a hundred different directions—and I was absently answering with half-hearted responses. "God lives in heaven. God doesn't require sleep. Of course He does."

And then, she asked a question that made me *really* think.

"Mom, does God cry?"

As I thought about how I would respond, my throat grew tight. My child—my three-year-old—was looking at God in a way I hadn't in a long time. She was looking at Him as more than a faceless entity in the sky. As more than a vending machine for my needs and requests. As more than an angry disciplinarian waiting to make me pay. She was looking at God as capable of emotion, thought, life, and complexity.

She was looking at God *as God*.

Tears blurred my vision. I needed the perspective of my three-year-old child. I needed to be reminded that God is personal. That He is real. My daughter's insatiable thirst for knowledge helped me view my world differently. That's the beauty of a mind that isn't afraid to ask, "*Why?*"

In this new, curious stage, you are the architect of your child's perception. You get the opportunity to shape and mold a mind that is maturing and growing at an incredible rate of speed. You are teaching your child lessons they'll remember for the rest of their lives. And in turn, maybe they're teaching you some things, too.

**- SUE MILLER**
*EXECUTIVE DIRECTOR OF VOLUNTEER STRATEGY FOR ORANGE, AUTHOR, INTERNATIONAL SPEAKER, & GRANDMOTHER*

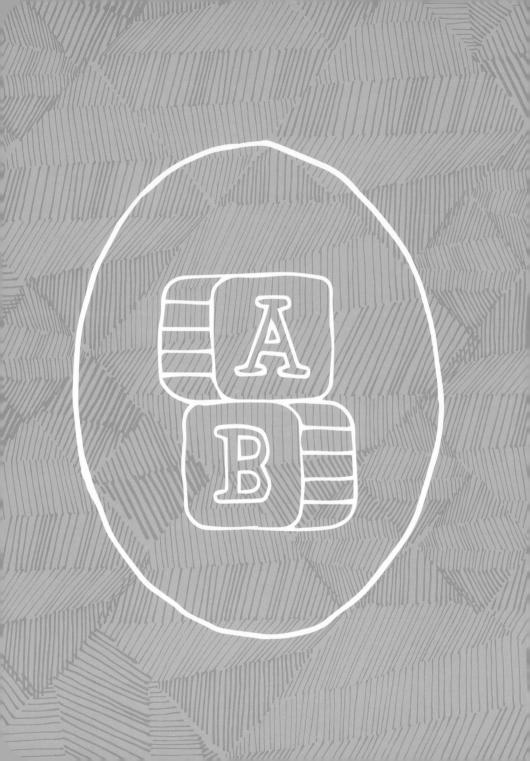

# SECTION ONE

—

# 52 WEEKS

## TO PARENT YOUR

## THREE-YEAR-OLD

WHEN YOU SEE
HOW MUCH

*Time*

YOU HAVE LEFT

—

YOU TEND TO DO

*More*

WITH THE TIME
YOU HAVE NOW.

THERE ARE APPROXIMATELY
# 936 WEEKS
## FROM THE TIME A BABY IS BORN UNTIL THEY GROW UP AND MOVE TO WHATEVER IS NEXT.

It may seem hard to believe, but at least 156 of those weeks have already passed you by. And while the future still feels far away, you're probably beginning to realize your kid is growing up faster than you ever dreamed.

That's why every week counts. Of course, each week might not feel significant. There may be weeks this year when all you feel like you accomplished was enduring an epic preschool tantrum. That's okay.

Take a deep breath.
You don't have to get everything done this week.

But what happens in your child's life week after week, year after year, adds up over time. So, it might be a good idea to put a number to your weeks.

## MEASURE IT OUT.

Write down the number of weeks that have already passed since your preschooler was born. Then write down the number of weeks you have left before they graduate high school.

🔒 **HINT:** If you want a little help counting it out, you can download the free Parent Cue app on all mobile platforms.

_____

_____

_____

## CREATE A VISUAL COUNTDOWN.

 Find a jar and fill it with one marble for each week you have remaining with your child. Then make a habit of removing one marble every week as a reminder to make the most of your time you have with your child.

Where can you place your visual countdown so you will see it frequently?

_____

_____

_____

_____

Which day of the week is best for you to remove a marble?

_____

_____

_____

Is there anything you want to do each week as you remove a marble? (Examples: say a prayer, write in a baby book, retell one favorite memory from this past week)

_____

_____

_____

_____

_____

_____

_____

_____

_____

_____

_____

EVERY PHASE IS A
TIMEFRAME
IN A KID'S LIFE
WHEN YOU CAN
LEVERAGE
DISTINCTIVE
OPPORTUNITIES
TO INFLUENCE
THEIR
*future.*

# YOU ONLY HAVE
# 52 WEEKS
## WITH YOUR THREE-YEAR-OLD

*while they are still three.*

Then they will be four,

*and you will never know them as a three-year-old again.*

That might be incredibly emotional,

or it might be the best news you've heard all day.

---

Or to say it another way:

Before you know it, your preschooler will grow up a little more and . . .

make their own breakfast.

swing by themselves.

brush their own teeth.

---

Just remember, the phase you are in now has remarkable potential.
Before their fourth birthday, there are some distinctive opportunities
you don't want to miss. So, as you count down the next 52 weeks,
pay attention to what makes these weeks different from the rest of
the weeks you will have with your child as they grow.

**What are some things you have noticed about your three-year-old in this phase that you really enjoy?**

_____

_____

_____

_____

_____

_____

_____

_____

_____

_____

_____

_____

_____

_____

_____

_____

_____

_____

_____

_____

**What is something new you are learning as a parent during this phase?**

_____

_____

_____

_____

_____

_____

_____

_____

_____

_____

_____

_____

_____

_____

_____

_____

_____

_____

_____

_____

# THREE

---

## THE PHASE WHEN ANYTHING CAN BE IMAGINED, EVERYTHING CAN BE A GAME, AND ONE CURIOUS PRESCHOOLER WANTS TO KNOW,

### "Why?"

## IMAGINATION IS REALITY.

Your three-year-old might suddenly become a self-proclaimed princess, pirate, or superhero. Your bedroom might turn out to be a train station, a castle, or both. But imagination may also turn scary. Fear may set in when, at any given moment, a monster can show up in the hallway, a snake can be under the bed, or a dragon can walk through the living room.

## EVERYTHING CAN BE A GAME.

You motivate your preschooler best when you appeal to their desire to play. Whatever the task, turn it into a game; make it fun. When you're having fun, they'll have fun with you. And there is simply nothing more entertaining than the spontaneous laughter of a three-year-old.

## THEY HAVE A NEWFOUND CURIOSITY.

Whether it's showcased in unrolling the toilet paper, pulling apart an older kid's LEGOs®, or the constant repetition of "Why? Why? Why?", your preschooler is eager to know how the world works. So when they ask you "Why?" for the second and third time, remember they're just looking for more of the knowledge they know you must have.

YOUR
THREE-
YEAR-
OLD
IS
*changing.*

## PHYSICALLY

- Balances on one foot for 5-10 seconds
- Strings beads and cuts with scissors (the plastic kind)
- Walks up stairs with alternating feet
- Puts on shoes (Just don't try to correct them if they put the left on their right foot.)

## VERBALLY

- Increasingly easier to understand
- May struggle with some sounds: r, l, s, z, j, sh, ch, th
- Says over 1,000 words (but who's really counting anymore?)
- Answers "what", "where", and "when" questions

## MENTALLY

- May struggle to understand "real" from "not real"
- Unable to take the point of view of others
- Lives in the present; has a limited memory of past events
- Learns by putting things into simple categories

## EMOTIONALLY

- May scream, throw tantrums, and show aggression
- Enjoys both physical humor and simple jokes
- Can express basic emotions when asked
- Can tell you what makes them happy or sad

**What are some changes you are noticing in your three-year-old?**

_____

_____

_____

_____

_____

_____

_____

**You may disagree with some of the characteristics we've shared about three-year-olds. That's because every three-year-old is unique. What makes your three-year-old different from three-year-olds in general?**

_____

_____

_____

_____

_____

_____

_____

_____

**What do you want to remember about this year with your three-year-old?**

Mark this page. Throughout the year, write down a few simple things that you want to remember. If you want to be really thorough, there are about 52 blank lines. But some weeks, you may be trying to clean Sharpie® off the wall and miss out on writing down a memory. That's okay.

_____

_____

_____

_____

_____

_____

_____

_____

_____

_____

_____

_____

_____

_____

_____

_____

_____

_____

# SECTION TWO
—
# SIX THINGS
EVERY KID

NEEDS

YOUR KID **NEEDS** **6** **THINGS** OVER TIME

LOVE

WORDS

WORK

PEOPLE

STORIES

FUN

# OVER THE NEXT 780 WEEKS, YOUR CHILD WILL NEED MANY THINGS.

Some of the things your kid needs will change from phase to phase, but there are six things that every kid needs at every phase. In fact, these things may be the most important things you give your kid—other than food. Kids need food.

**EVERY KID, AT EVERY PHASE, NEEDS . . .**

**LOVE**
to give them a
sense of WORTH.

**STORIES**
to give them a bigger
PERSPECTIVE.

**WORK**
to give them
PURPOSE.

**FUN**
to give them
CONNECTION.

**PEOPLE**
to give them
BELONGING.

**WORDS**
to give them
DIRECTION.

The next few pages are designed to help you think about how you can give these things to your three-year-old—before they turn four.

EVERY KID

NEEDS

*love*

OVER TIME

—

TO GIVE THEM

A SENSE OF

*worth.*

# ♡ ONE QUESTION YOUR THREE-YEAR-OLD IS ASKING

Life for your three-year-old can be confusing. It's okay to throw a ball, but not a rock. You can hug your friend, but not squeeze his neck. Your three-year-old is learning the rules for life and encountering some necessary discipline.

Your preschooler is asking one major question:

## "AM I OKAY?"

Your preschooler needs to know you love them—even when they make bad choices. As the parent of a three-year-old who may test your limits on a daily (or hourly) basis, you may feel overwhelmed at times. But remember this, in order to give your three-year-old the love and discipline they need, you need to do one thing:

## EMBRACE their physical needs.

When you embrace your three-year-old's needs, you . . .
communicate that they are safe,
establish that the world can be trusted,
and demonstrate that they are worth loving.

You are probably doing more than you realize to show your three-year-old how much you love them. Make a list of the ways you already show up to consistently embrace your preschooler's physical needs.

You may need to look at this list on a bad day to remember what a great parent you are.

_____

_____

_____

_____

_____

_____

_____

_____

_____

_____

_____

_____

_____

Showing love requires paying attention to what someone likes.
What does your three-year-old seem to enjoy the most
right now?

_____

_____

_____

_____

_____

_____

_____

_____

_____

_____

_____

_____

_____

_____

_____

_____

_____

_____

It's impossible to love anyone with the relentless effort a three-year-old demands unless you have a little time for yourself. What can you do to refuel each week so you are able to give your preschooler the love they need?

_____

_____

_____

_____

_____

_____

_____

_____

_____

_____

_____

_____

_____

_____

_____

_____

_____

_____

**Who do you have around you supporting you this year?**

_____

_____

_____

_____

_____

_____

_____

_____

_____

_____

_____

_____

_____

_____

_____

_____

_____

_____

_____

_____

_____

_____

EVERY KID

NEEDS

*stories*

OVER TIME

—

TO GIVE THEM

A BIGGER

*perspective.*

# BOOKS TO READ WITH YOUR THREE-YEAR OLD

**MOONCAKE**
by Frank Asch

**SAM AND DAVE DIG A HOLE**
by Mac Barnett and Jon Klassen

**MADELINE**
by Ludwig Bemelmans

**MR. GUMPY'S OUTING**
by John Burningham

**MIKE MULLIGAN AND
HIS STEAM SHOVEL**
by Virginia Lee Burton

**STREGA NONA (SERIES)**
by Tomie dePaola

**BEAR SNORES ON**
by Karma Wilson
illustrated by Jane Chapman

**CORDUROY (SERIES)**
by Don Freeman

**HAROLD AND THE
PURPLE CRAYON**
by Crockett Johnson

**PETE THE CAT (SERIES)**
by Eric Litwin and James Dean

**MARTHA SPEAKS**
by Susan Meddaugh

**THE LITTLE ENGINE THAT COULD**
by Watty Piper

**GREEN EGGS AND HAM**
by Dr. Seuss

**THERE'S A WOCKET
IN MY POCKET!**
by Dr. Seuss

**PRESS HERE**
by Herve Tullet

**KNUFFLE BUNNY**
by Mo Willems

**IN MY HEART: A BOOK OF
FEELINGS**
by Jo Witek

**WHAT TO DO WITH A BOX**
by Jane Yolen
illustrated by Chris Sheban

**HARRY THE DIRTY DOG**
by Gene Zion

**THE POUT-POUT FISH**
by Deborah Diesen

Kids need the kind of stories you will read to them over time. But they also need family stories. What can you do this year to capture your family's story so you can retell the story of this year to your child when they are older?

_____

_____

_____

_____

_____

_____

_____

_____

_____

_____

_____

_____

_____

_____

_____

_____

_____

**What makes your family history unique? How can you preserve the story of your family's history for your child?**

_____

_____

_____

_____

_____

_____

_____

_____

_____

_____

_____

_____

_____

_____

_____

_____

_____

_____

_____

_____

Are there other stories that matter to you? What are they, and how will you share those stories with your preschooler?

_____

_____

_____

_____

_____

_____

_____

_____

_____

_____

_____

_____

_____

_____

_____

_____

_____

EVERY KID

NEEDS

*work*

OVER TIME

—

TO GIVE

THEM

*purpose.*

# WORK YOUR
# THREE-YEAR-OLD CAN DO

**USE THE POTTY**

**USE A FORK AND SPOON**

**TAKE TRASH TO
THE TRASH CAN**

**FILL A PET'S FOOD OR
WATER DISH**

**DRESS THEMSELVES**
(kind of)

**PICK UP TOYS**

**PUT DIRTY CLOTHES IN
THE HAMPER**

**CARRY DISHES
TO THE SINK**

**HELP CARRY GROCERIES**
(the light ones)

**PUT GROCERIES ON THE
CONVEYOR BELT**

**WATER PLANTS**
(when you ask)

**What are some things your three-year-old has worked to accomplish so far?**

_____

_____

_____

_____

_____

_____

_____

_____

_____

_____

_____

_____

_____

_____

_____

_____

_____

How are you giving your three-year-old opportunities to help out at home? What do you do to reward their efforts?

_____

_____

_____

_____

_____

_____

_____

_____

_____

_____

_____

_____

_____

_____

_____

_____

_____

**What are some things you hope your preschooler will be able to do independently in the next phase?**

_____

_____

_____

_____

_____

_____

_____

_____

_____

_____

_____

_____

_____

_____

_____

_____

_____

_____

_____

_____

_____

**How are you helping them develop those skills now?**

_____

_____

_____

_____

_____

_____

_____

_____

_____

_____

_____

_____

_____

_____

_____

_____

_____

_____

_____

_____

_____

_____

EVERY KID

NEEDS

*fun*

OVER TIME

—

TO GIVE

THEM

*connection.*

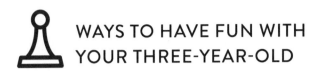

# WAYS TO HAVE FUN WITH YOUR THREE-YEAR-OLD

## TOYS:

**PLAY-DOH®**

**FINGER PAINT**

**CRAYONS**

**PLAY KITCHEN**

**ALPHABET LETTERS**

**DUPLO LEGOS®**

**WOODEN PUZZLES**

**TRUCKS, TRAINS, AND DOLLS**

## ACTIVITIES:

**DRESS UP CLOTHES**

**PUSH A SWING**

**THROW OR KICK A BALL**

**BLOW BUBBLES**

**DO A SILLY DANCE**

**PLAY FREEZE GAMES**

**PLAY "MOTHER MAY I?"**

**PLAY "MUSICAL CHAIRS"**

**PLAY "DUCK, DUCK, GOOSE"**

**SING "ITSY-BITSY-SPIDER"**

**SING "LONDON BRIDGES"**

**What are some activities that make you and your three-year-old laugh?**

_____

_____

_____

_____

_____

_____

_____

_____

_____

_____

_____

_____

_____

_____

_____

_____

_____

_____

**When are the best times of the day, or week, for you to set aside to have fun with your three-year-old?**

_____

_____

_____

_____

_____

_____

_____

_____

_____

_____

_____

_____

_____

_____

_____

_____

_____

_____

_____

What are some ways you want to celebrate the special days coming up this year?

# 4TH BIRTHDAY

_____

_____

_____

_____

_____

_____

_____

_____

_____

_____

_____

_____

_____

_____

_____

_____

_____

# HOLIDAYS

_____
_____
_____
_____
_____
_____
_____
_____
_____
_____
_____
_____
_____
_____
_____
_____
_____
_____
_____
_____
_____
_____

EVERY KID

NEEDS

*people*

OVER TIME

—

TO GIVE

THEM

*belonging.*

# ADULTS WHO MIGHT INFLUENCE YOUR THREE-YEAR-OLD

**PARENTS**

**PARENT'S FRIENDS**

**GRANDPARENTS**

**NURSERY WORKERS**

**AUNTS AND UNCLES**

**BABYSITTERS OR NANNIES**

List at least five adults who have influence in your three-year-old's life right now.

HINT: They're probably the adults your three-year-old talks about.

_____

_____

_____

_____

_____

_____

_____

_____

_____

_____

_____

_____

_____

_____

_____

_____

_____

_____

_____

**What is one way these adults could help you and your preschooler this year?**

EXAMPLES: pray for you, play with your three-year-old, watch older siblings so you can play with the three-year-old

_____

_____

_____

_____

_____

_____

_____

_____

_____

_____

_____

_____

_____

_____

_____

_____

**What are a few ways you could show these adults appreciation for the significant role they play in your child's life?**

_____

_____

_____

_____

_____

_____

_____

_____

_____

_____

_____

_____

_____

_____

_____

_____

_____

_____

EVERY KID

NEEDS

*words*

OVER TIME

—

TO GIVE

THEM

*direction.*

# WORDS YOUR THREE-YEAR-OLD NEEDS TO HEAR

The best way to begin preparing your three-year-old for school is by improving their vocabulary. Here are a few suggestions:

| 1. | 2. | 3. | 4. | 5. |
|---|---|---|---|---|
| Talk to your preschooler —the more, the better. | When they talk, make eye contact. | Give your preschooler opportunities to make choices. | Read, sing, or make up rhymes. | Join your child in pretend play. |

What word (or words) describe your hopes for your child in this phase?

| | | |
|---|---|---|
| DETERMINED | MOTIVATED | GENTLE |
| ENCOURAGING | INTROSPECTIVE | PASSIONATE |
| SELF-ASSURED | ENTHUSIASTIC | PATIENT |
| ASSERTIVE | JOYFUL | FORGIVING |
| DARING | ENTERTAINING | CREATIVE |
| INSIGHTFUL | INDEPENDENT | WITTY |
| COMPASSIONATE | OBSERVANT | AMBITIOUS |
| AMIABLE | SENSITIVE | HELPFUL |
| EASY-GOING | ENDEARING | AUTHENTIC |
| DILIGENT | ADVENTUROUS | INVENTIVE |
| PROACTIVE | HONEST | DEVOTED |
| OPTIMISTIC | CURIOUS | GENUINE |
| FEARLESS | DEPENDABLE | ATTENTIVE |
| AFFECTIONATE | GENEROUS | HARMONIOUS |
| COURAGEOUS | COMMITTED | EMPATHETIC |
| CAUTIOUS | RESPONSIBLE | COURAGEOUS |
| DEVOTED | TRUSTWORTHY | FLEXIBLE |
| INQUISITIVE | THOUGHTFUL | CAREFUL |
| PATIENT | LOYAL | NURTURING |
| OPEN-MINDED | KIND | RELIABLE |

**Where can you place those words in your home so they will remind you what you want for your child this year?**

_____

_____

_____

_____

_____

_____

_____

_____

_____

_____

_____

_____

_____

_____

_____

_____

_____

_____

_____

_____

Don't be surprised if you find yourself fighting not to laugh out loud at some of the incredible things your three-year-old says this year. Write them down. The words of your three-year-old can become the stuff of great family stories for years to come.

_____

_____

_____

_____

_____

_____

_____

_____

_____

_____

_____

_____

_____

_____

_____

_____

_____

_____

# SECTION THREE

—

# FOUR CONVERSATIONS

## TO HAVE IN THIS PHASE

WHEN YOU KNOW
WHERE YOU WANT
TO GO,

AND YOU KNOW
WHERE YOU ARE
NOW,

YOU CAN ALWAYS
DO SOMETHING

TO MOVE IN A
BETTER DIRECTION.

# OVER THE NEXT 780 WEEKS OF YOUR CHILD'S LIFE, SOME CONVERSATIONS MAY MATTER MORE THAN OTHERS.

**WHAT YOU SAY, FOR EXAMPLE, REGARDING . . .**

Pirates

Spiders

and Football

**MIGHT HAVE LESS IMPACT ON THEIR FUTURE THAN WHAT YOU SAY REGARDING . . .**

Health

Sex

Technology

or Faith.

The next pages are about the conversations that matter most. On the left page is a destination—what you might want to be true in your kid's life 780 weeks from now. On the right page is a goal for conversations with your three-year-old and a few suggestions about what you might want to say.

# Healthy habits

—

## LEARNING TO STRENGTHEN MY BODY THROUGH EXERCISE, NUTRITION, AND SELF-ADVOCACY

**THIS YEAR YOU WILL**

# ESTABLISH BASIC NUTRITION

**SO YOUR CHILD WILL HAVE CONSISTENT CARE AND EXPERIENCE A VARIETY OF FOOD.**

Maintain a good relationship with your pediatrician, and schedule a well visit at least once per year. You can also begin to build a foundation of healthy habits for your three-year-old with a few simple words.

**SAY THINGS LIKE . . .**

TIME TO BRUSH YOUR TEETH!

HERE'S YOUR MILK.

LET'S GO OUTSIDE.

IT'S OKAY IF YOU DON'T LIKE YOUR PEAS TODAY, YOU MIGHT LIKE THEM NEXT TIME.

DID YOU KNOW CARROTS GROW UNDERGROUND?

THANK YOU FOR TRYING THAT.

CAN YOU HELP ME COOK?

LET'S WASH YOUR HANDS.

**What can you do this year to help your three-year-old exercise?** *(Okay, "exercise" may be a stretch, but climbing and sliding and swinging count.)*

_____

_____

_____

_____

_____

_____

_____

_____

_____

_____

_____

_____

_____

_____

_____

_____

_____

_____

What are some ways you might try to improve your three-year-old's nutrition? Do they eat vegetables and fruit regularly?

_____

_____

_____

_____

_____

_____

_____

_____

_____

_____

_____

_____

_____

_____

_____

_____

_____

_____

_____

_____

_____

**Who will help you monitor and improve your three-year-old's health this year?**

_____

_____

_____

_____

_____

_____

_____

_____

_____

_____

_____

_____

_____

_____

_____

_____

_____

_____

_____

What are your own health goals for this year? How can you improve the habits in your own life—even though you might already be getting more exercise than ever just trying to keep pace?

_____

_____

_____

_____

_____

_____

_____

_____

_____

_____

_____

_____

_____

_____

_____

_____

_____

_____

# Sexual integrity

—

GUARDING MY
POTENTIAL FOR
INTIMACY THROUGH
APPROPRIATE
BOUNDARIES
AND MUTUAL
RESPECT

THIS YEAR YOU WILL
# INTRODUCE THEM TO THEIR BODY
SO YOUR CHILD WILL DISCOVER THEIR BODY
AND DEFINE PRIVACY.

There's a good chance your preschooler is becoming more aware of their body and the bodies of others. Use this time to lay a foundation for future conversations by simply talking about bodies in a positive way.

**SAY THINGS LIKE . . .**

**CLOSE THE DOOR WHEN YOU GO TO THE POTTY.**

**THAT'S YOUR NOSE. THOSE ARE YOUR EYES. THAT'S YOUR VAGINA / PENIS.**
(Help your child learn the correct names of body parts. Experts suggest that learning proper words can protect your kid from potential harm as well as create a positive view of their body.)

**I LOVE WATCHING YOU GROW.**

**NO, GIRLS DON'T HAVE A PENIS.**
(If your child notices that someone's body is different than their own, talk about the differences.)

**BABIES GROW INSIDE THEIR MAMA UNTIL IT'S TIME TO BE BORN.**

**What influences shaped your views of sex growing up?** *(parents, media, friends, other adults . . . )*

_____

_____

_____

_____

_____

_____

_____

_____

_____

_____

_____

_____

_____

_____

_____

_____

_____

_____

_____

How does your own life story shape your future hopes for your child in this area?

_____

_____

_____

_____

_____

_____

_____

_____

_____

_____

_____

_____

_____

_____

_____

_____

_____

_____

_____

_____

_____

When it comes to your child's sexuality, what do you hope is true for them 780 weeks from now?

_____

_____

_____

_____

_____

_____

_____

_____

_____

_____

_____

_____

_____

_____

_____

_____

_____

_____

_____

_____

Are you and your spouse, or your child's other parent, on the same page when it comes to talking about sex with your child? How might you work on a plan to communicate your hopes, expectations, and real-time conversations with your child about sex?

_____

_____

_____

_____

_____

_____

_____

_____

_____

_____

_____

_____

_____

_____

_____

_____

# Technological responsibility

—

## LEVERAGING THE POTENTIAL OF ONLINE EXPERIENCES TO ENHANCE MY OFFLINE COMMUNITY AND SUCCESS

THIS YEAR YOU WILL
# ENJOY THE ADVANTAGES
SO YOUR CHILD WILL EXPERIENCE BOUNDARIES
AND HAVE POSITIVE EXPOSURE.

One advantage to technology is that you probably already have a resident expert who navigates a tablet faster than some adults. But since three-year-olds are drawn to a screen, it's also time to have a few conversations about digital devices.

**SAY THINGS LIKE . . .**

**I'M TEXTING GRANDMA TO ASK A QUESTION.**
(Talk openly about technology as you use it.)

**I PUT MY PHONE AWAY WHEN WE ARE EATING SO WE CAN TALK TO EACH OTHER.**
(Set limits for screen time.)

**IT'S TIME FOR YOU TO PUT THE IPAD AWAY.**

**YOU NEED TO ASK BEFORE YOU USE THE COMPUTER.**
(Know when they are on a device and what they are using it to do.)

**LET ME SHOW YOU WHAT A DOLPHIN LOOKS LIKE.**
(Use technology to enhance your conversations.)

What kind of digital access was available to you when you were growing up? How have things changed since then?

_____

_____

_____

_____

_____

_____

_____

_____

_____

_____

_____

_____

_____

_____

_____

_____

_____

_____

_____

_____

What are some issues you think may come up as you raise your child in a digitally connected world? Where can you go to find advice to help navigate those issues?

_____

_____

_____

_____

_____

_____

_____

_____

_____

_____

_____

_____

_____

_____

_____

_____

_____

**When it comes to your child's engagement with technology, what do you hope is true for them 780 weeks from now?**

_____

_____

_____

_____

_____

_____

_____

_____

_____

_____

_____

_____

_____

_____

_____

_____

_____

_____

_____

_____

_____

What are your own personal values and disciplines when it comes to leveraging technology? Are there ways you want to improve your own savvy, skill, or responsibility in this area?

_____

_____

_____

_____

_____

_____

_____

_____

_____

_____

_____

_____

_____

_____

_____

_____

_____

_____

_____

# Authentic
# faith

—

TRUSTING JESUS
IN A WAY THAT
TRANSFORMS HOW
I LOVE GOD,
MYSELF,
AND THE REST
OF THE WORLD

## THIS YEAR YOU WILL
# INCITE WONDER
## SO YOUR CHILD WILL KNOW GOD'S LOVE
## AND MEET GOD'S FAMILY.

Your three-year-old has many questions. Some might be about creation, heaven, church, and the Bible . . . and some of their questions might already be hard to answer. Don't panic. Just like other topics, answer faith questions as simply as possible. If they need to ask more, they will.

**SAY THINGS LIKE . . .**

**GOD MADE YOU. GOD LOVES YOU. JESUS WANTS TO BE YOUR FRIEND FOREVER.**

**HOW DID THE SAMARITAN TAKE CARE OF HIS NEIGHBOR?**
(Talk about what your preschooler learns at church.)

**"WITH GOD ALL THINGS ARE POSSIBLE."** Matthew 19:26
(Repeat simple Bible verses.)

**ARE YOU SCARED? LET'S TALK TO GOD ABOUT IT.**

**CAN YOU LET YOUR FRIEND HAVE A TURN?**
(Prompt them to share.)

**ISN'T THAT WONDERFUL? LET'S THANK GOD FOR IT.**

**Who will help you develop your child's faith as they grow?**

_____

_____

_____

_____

_____

_____

_____

_____

_____

_____

_____

_____

_____

_____

_____

_____

_____

_____

_____

_____

Is there a volunteer at your church who shows up consistently each week for your child? Do you attend a consistent service so your kid knows who will greet them each week?

_____

_____

_____

_____

_____

_____

_____

_____

_____

_____

_____

_____

_____

_____

_____

_____

_____

_____

_____

**When it comes to your child's faith, what do you hope is true for them 780 weeks from now?**

_____

_____

_____

_____

_____

_____

_____

_____

_____

_____

_____

_____

_____

_____

_____

_____

_____

_____

_____

_____

**What routines or habits do you have in your own life that are stretching your faith?**

_____

_____

_____

_____

_____

_____

_____

_____

_____

_____

_____

_____

_____

_____

_____

_____

_____

_____

_____

THE

*rhythm*

OF YOUR

WEEK

—

WILL SHAPE

THE VALUES

IN YOUR

*home.*

# NOW THAT YOU HAVE FILLED THIS BOOK WITH DREAMS, IDEAS, AND GOALS, IT MAY SEEM AS IF YOU WILL NEVER HAVE TIME TO GET IT ALL DONE.

Actually, you have *780 weeks*.

And every week has potential.

The secret to making the most of this phase with your three-year-old is to take advantage of the time you already have. Create a rhythm to your weeks by leveraging these four times together.

Set the mood for the day. Smile. Greet them with words of love.

Reinforce simple ideas. Talk to your preschooler and play music as you go.

Be personal. Spend one-on-one time that communicates love and affection.

Wind down together. Provide comfort as the day draws to a close.

## What seem to be your three-year-old's best times of the day?

---

**What are some of your favorite routines with your three-year-old?**

_____

_____

_____

_____

_____

_____

_____

_____

_____

_____

_____

_____

_____

_____

_____

_____

_____

_____

_____

_____

Write down any other thoughts or questions that you have about parenting your three-year-old.

_____

_____

_____

_____

_____

_____

_____

_____

_____

_____

_____

_____

_____

_____

_____

_____

_____

_____

_____

_____
_____
_____
_____
_____
_____
_____
_____
_____
_____
_____
_____
_____
_____
_____
_____
_____
_____
_____
_____
_____
_____
_____
_____
_____
_____

Maisie

IT'S JUST
A PHASE
SO DON'T
MISS IT.

# ABOUT THE AUTHORS

**KRISTEN IVY** @kristen_ivy

Kristen Ivy is executive director of the Phase Project. She and her husband, Matt, are in the preschool and elementary phases with three kids: Sawyer, Hensley, and Raleigh.

Kristen earned her Bachelors of Education from Baylor University in 2004 and received a Master of Divinity from Mercer University in 2009. She worked in the public school system as a high school biology and English teacher, where she learned firsthand the importance of influencing the next generation.

Kristen is also the President at Orange and has played an integral role in the development of the elementary, middle school, and high school curriculum and has shared her experiences at speaking events across the country. She is the co-author of *Playing for Keeps*, *Creating a Lead Small Culture*, *It's Just a Phase*, and *Don't Miss It*.

**REGGIE JOINER** @reggiejoiner

Reggie Joiner is founder and CEO of the reThink Group and co-founder of the Phase Project. He and his wife, Debbie, have reared four kids into adulthood. They now also have two grandchildren.

The reThink Group (also known as Orange) is a non-profit organization whose purpose is to influence those who influence the next generation. Orange provides resources and training for churches and organizations that create environments for parents, kids, and teenagers.

Before starting the reThink Group in 2006, Reggie was one of the founders of North Point Community Church. During his 11 years with Andy Stanley, Reggie was the executive director of family ministry, where he developed a new concept for relevant ministry to children, teenagers, and married adults. Reggie has authored and co-authored more than 10 books including: *Think Orange, Seven Practices of Effective Ministry, Parenting Beyond Your Capacity, Playing for Keeps, Lead Small, Creating a Lead Small Culture,* and his latest, *A New Kind of Leader* and *Don't Miss It.*

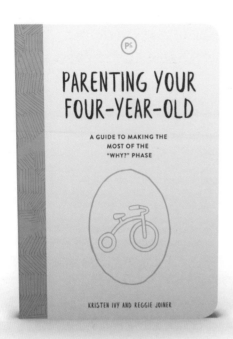

# MAKE THE MOST OF EVERY PHASE IN YOUR CHILD'S LIFE

**The guide in your hand is one of an eighteen-part series.**

So, unless you've figured out a way to freeze time and keep your three-year-old from turning into a four-year-old, you might want to check out the next guide in this set.

Designed in partnership with Parent Cue, each guide will help you rediscover . . .

what's changing about your kid,
the 6 things your kid needs most,
and 4 conversations to have each year.

**WANT TO GIFT A FRIEND WITH ALL 18 GUIDES
OR HAVE ALL THE GUIDES ON HAND FOR YOURSELF?**

# ORDER THE ENTIRE SERIES
# OF PHASE GUIDES TODAY.